# HIGH ABOVE JORDAN

Dedicated with admiration to
*HIS MAJESTY KING HUSSEIN I*
*by gracious permission*

First published in Jordan in 1989

ISBN 0 9512766 2 X

Designed and produced by
Three's Company
12 Flitcroft Street
London WC2H 8DJ
Great Britain

Co-edition organised and
produced by
Angus Hudson Ltd
66/73 Shoe Lane
London EC4P 4AB

Typesetting by Watermark, Watford

Printed in Great Britain by
Purnell Book Production Ltd
Paulton, Bristol

This book has been made possible through the generous support of

The Office of His Majesty King Hussein
The Office of the Prime Minister
The Ministry of Tourism
The Royal Jordanian Air Force
Royal Jordanian Airlines
Arab Bank
Petra Bank
Arab Jordan Investment Bank
Jordan Bank
National Finance Investment Bank

**Kerak Crusader Castle, ten miles south of the Dead Sea peninsula.**

# HIGH ABOVE JORDAN

## AERIAL PHOTOGRAPHS BY JANE TAYLOR
## FOREWORD BY H.M. KING HUSSEIN

*The Hashemite Kingdom of Jordan, our country, is the privileged home of some of the greatest monuments of human civilization. The Jordanian people are the proud custodians of these landmarks that testify to various epochs of recorded history. Petra, Wadi Rum, Jerash, to cite but a few examples, have been viewed and appreciated by millions here and from afar. Even our desert has its enchantments, with its Umayyad castles, and the wildlife sanctuaries that house some of the rarest species of the animal kingdom. Historians, explorers, archaeologists, travel writers and film-makers have brought this glorious heritage to the attention of the world.*

*Through the relatively recent art of aerial photography, Jane Taylor is seeking to convey the majestic splendour of these treasures. She has succeeded in this almost impossible task. I say this since no narrative text or photographic portrayal can do justice to these landmarks. Only personal visits and contact can convey the enduring spirit and inspiring message that these treasures carry from bygone times and generations. I hope that readers of this book will be prompted to make this journey.*

*Ahlan wa Sahlan — you will be truly at home among our people.*

*Hussein I*

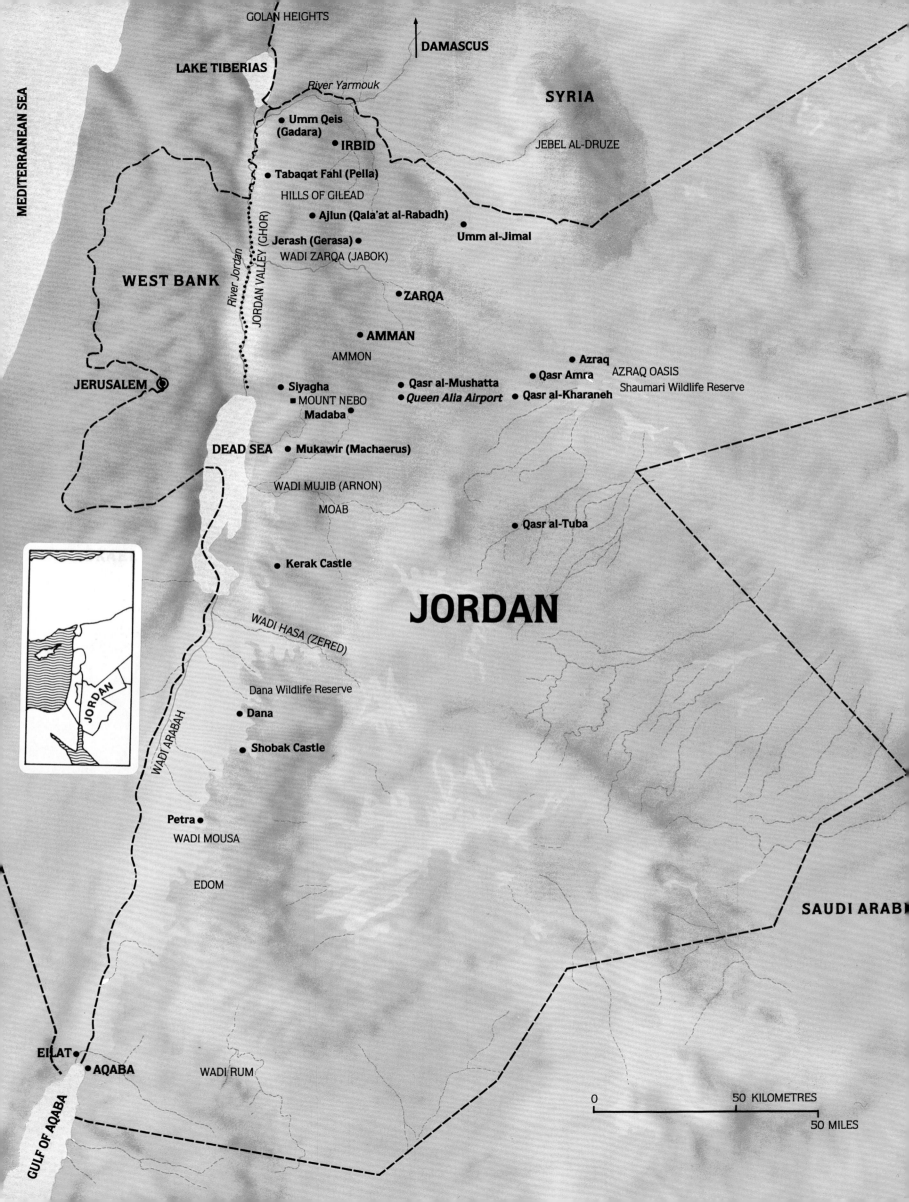

# CONTENTS

Introduction
8

Acknowledgments
11

Amman
12

Amman, the Roman Theatre
14

Jerash, Gerasa
16

Ajlun, Qala'at al-Rabadh
18

Umm Qeis, Gadara
20

The Hills of Gilead
22

Tabaqat Fahl, Pella
24

Umm al-Jimal
26

Azraq Oasis
28

Qasr al-Tuba
30

Qasr Amra
32

Qasr al-Kharaneh
34

Qasr al-Mushatta
36

Madaba
38

Mount Nebo
40

Machaerus
42

Petra, the 'Rock'
44

The Rediscovery of Petra
46

Petra, the Rose-red City
48

The High Places of Petra
50

A Bedouin Encampment
52

Wadi Rum
54

Aqaba
56

Shobak Crusader Castle
58

Dana
60

Kerak Crusader Castle
62

Index
64

# Introduction

When Western travellers first ventured cautiously into this barely-known territory east of the river Jordan, early in the nineteenth century, they were astonished to find landscapes of breath-taking beauty and variety. They marvelled at wild mountains and wilder canyons, the deepest gorge on earth, hot springs, green forests and fruitful valleys, the weird formations of the Dead Sea and the stark aridity of the desert.

In the midst of all this they might happen upon a Hellenistic palace; a Roman city still entire, or a single theatre; and a multitude of Byzantine churches with wonderful mosaics. Umayyad palaces were chanced upon, scattered almost prodigally in the desert, adorned with vivid frescoes or delicate carving. And in the hills they found not only some of the mightiest castles of the Crusaders, but another fortress, equally grand, built by the Arabs in their stand against the Christian invaders. Prize discovery of all was the fabled city of the Nabataeans, lost for centuries to all but a handful of bedu, but found in 1812 by the Swiss explorer John Burckhardt — Petra.

Once Burckhardt's discovery was made known, the trickle of tourists became a steady stream, each person hoping for some immortalizing find of his own. From all over Europe and America they came, travelling widely and often uncomfortably, some armed with the Bible as their travel guide, others with Strabo, Pliny or Josephus. Several painted as they went — some magnificently, like David Roberts whose paintings of Petra and other places opened still more Western eyes to the glories of this area of earth. An even greater number wrote books — to such an extent that it became fashionable to preface yet another volume of travel in the Middle East with yet another excuse for writing it.

Today's traveller to Jordan still has this wealth of scenery and monuments, with the charm and generosity of the Jordanians to enliven the trip, and a near perfect climate in which to travel. Anywhere — even on patches of grass in the heart of modern Amman — you may find a shepherd with his flock of sheep and black goats; or, in biblical fashion, carrying on his shoulders one that is lame or left behind. Still, if you are lucky, you may see a group of bedouin on the move to summer pastures, their camels and flocks streaming through the vastness of an empty plain. At such moments it seems as if time has stood still.

## Earliest times

The land of Jordan, like all its close neighbours, has been inhabited by man since time immemorial. Palaeolithic, Neolithic, Chalcolithic, Bronze Age and Iron Age people occupied these hills, valleys and deserts, leaving tools and pots and other artefacts as witnesses to their lives. And for almost as long as the land has been occupied, travellers have passed through it, to trade, to conquer or to convert.

When Moses led his unruly Israelites into these territories, perhaps around 1270 BC, they found as they travelled north from Sinai three well-established kingdoms — Edom, Moab and Ammon — each with a culture and economy considerably more advanced than their own. It is hardly surprising that the king of Edom refused passage along the King's Highway, which passed through his lands, to these unpredictable wanderers; but the huge detour forced on the Jews did little for good neighbourly relations in the future. Aggression became endemic between the earlier inhabitants and the Israelites as lands were fought over, lost, and won again.

Even when the Jews finally settled west of the river Jordan, hostility remained the norm, though there were brief moments of tentative and unrepeated good nature. When King David was on the run from Saul, he was given sanctuary in Edom and Moab, and possibly Ammon; but this kindness did not deter him, after he became king, from attacking those kingdoms, slaughtering two-thirds of the people of Edom, and ordering the massacre of every Moabite male, of any age, that could be found.

The Assyrians came in about 800 BC and for the next 200 years dominated the land and its people by the imposition of governors and tribute. But in 612 Nineveh fell, and the Babylonian Empire replaced the Assyrian. The Babylonians, in their turn, were replaced in 539 by the Empire of the Persians, whose satraps governed the province until Alexander defeated them in 333 BC.

## The Hellenistic period

After Alexander's death his generals divided his new empire between them — Ptolemy took Egypt, Palestine, Jordan and southern Syria; and Seleucus took northern Syria. Judging his portion to be inadequate, Seleucus soon annexed southern Syria and Jordan, to be challenged a few years later by Ptolemy II, who wanted them back. Despite recurrent changes of hands between the Ptolemies and Seleucids, Jordan prospered, and Hellenistic art and culture breathed new life into existing oriental traditions — coins were minted similar to Greek ones; cities were built, or rebuilt, in the Greek style and given Greek names to match. Even the Nabataeans, remote in their wild mountainous regions to the south, were influenced by Greek styles of architecture.

Nobody is quite sure when the Nabataeans first appeared in the Edomite mountains. It may have been as early as around 580 BC, when the Edomites began to move into the more fertile lands west of Wadi Arabah. The first certain reference to them here is in 312 BC, when they were attacked by the Seleucid King Antigonus the One-eyed. By then they were already well established, with their capital at Petra, and had amassed enormous wealth from controlling the trade routes that passed through their territory. They also profited from the continuing conflict between the Ptolemies and Seleucids which enabled them to expand northwards, even reaching Damascus in the mid-first century BC.

**A chilli crop in the fertile Jordan valley. The Judean Hills can be seen in the distance.**

### Romans and Byzantines

By now a new empire-builder was active in the Middle East — Rome. In 63 BC Pompey secured Jordan and its cities, leaving them free to govern themselves, but obliged to pay taxes to Rome. Only the Nabataeans remained independent — at the price of a handsome present to keep the Romans away. It was Herod the Great, urged on by Mark Antony, who drove the Nabataeans out of the northern part of their kingdom, back to their heartland around Petra.

From this time on, the Romans imposed their rule over most of the area. East of the Jordan there were three separate districts — in the north the Decapolis, a region dominated by ten cities under the tutelage of Rome; in the centre Peraea, also Roman; in the south was the still independent kingdom of the Nabataeans. In AD 106, in the reign of the Emperor Trajan, Nabataean independence and its line of kings came to an end, and the territory became known as the Roman Province of Arabia. Prosperity continued throughout the province, more and more new towns and villages were built, and existing ones were made more glorious with new temples, baths and theatres.

When the Roman Emperor Constantine became a Christian in 312, Christianity became the most favoured religion; and in 395 it was institutionalized as the state religion of the emergent Byzantine Empire. Bishoprics were established, and churches replaced temples as the most popular new buildings of the day.

### The coming of Islam

In 636, only four years after the death of the Prophet Muhammad, an army of Arabs, filled with the fire of their new faith, defeated the mighty Byzantines at the battle of the river Yarmouk, on the northern border of Jordan. Soon afterwards the Umayyad caliphs established their capital at Damascus, and built a series of palaces and hunting lodges in the Jordanian desert. They stand there still, enchanting but tumbled pleasure domes, once the ultimate in beauty and fine craftsmanship and luxury. But the Umayyads were ousted by their scheming co-religionists of the Abbasid dynasty who in 763 transferred their capital to Baghdad, leaving Jordan to decline into insignificance, for even trade was now passing along other routes.

### The Crusaders

The largely unlovable Crusaders staged a return of Christianity in the early twelfth century, but they were driven out of Jerusalem and many of their possessions before the end of that century by the vastly more civilized and chivalrous Salah al-Din. In the following century the Mamluks marched in from Egypt, but in 1516 they fell to the thrusting empire of the Ottoman Turks.

For four hundred years Jordan remained a backwater of the Ottoman Empire. Europeans, who in the sixteenth and seventeenth centuries flocked to the Ottoman and Saffavid Empires in pursuit of new trade, ignored Jordan, for the great commercial centres were to the north, east and south — Constantinople, Aleppo, Isfahan and Cairo. Jordan's main significance, such as it was, came from the pilgrimage route which passed through it from Turkey to the Muslim holy places of Mecca and Medina. Then for a brief annual interlude the towns and countryside would come alive as the camels, horses, donkeys and people of the Haj caravan passed on their dusty, noisy way, providing an itinerant market for food, drink, accommodation and protection. When the Hejaz railway was built in the late nineteenth century, even this small passing trade was virtually eliminated.

### The Arab Revolt

It was the First World War that brought Jordan back into the mainstream of history; it was then that King Hussein of Jordan's remarkable great-grandfather, Sherif Hussein ibn Ali, Grand Emir of Mecca, King of the Hejaz, 37th in direct line of descent from the Prophet Muhammad, launched the legendary Arab Revolt against the Turks. It was led by his sons, the Emirs Feisal, Abdullah and Ali. The Arabs needed arms, money and expert advisers; the British needed help to break Germany's ally, Turkey. Accordingly the British promised the Arabs the lands and the independence they desired once the war was over. Outstanding among the British advisers was T.E.Lawrence who, with the Arab leaders, operated with great panache and success through the length and breadth of Jordan. With victory in 1918, the British and French set about re-drawing the Arab map, establishing their own mandate areas in flagrant disregard for British pledges of Arab independence.

### From Transjordan to Jordan

In 1921 Emir Feisal became King of Iraq, under British mandate; and Emir Abdullah, most original and vivid of the brothers, accepted the poorest and least productive country as his portion — Transjordan, its capital, Amman, then little more than a village with a few Roman ruins. It was not a kingdom, and it was not independent; but Abdullah transformed his country into the most united and disciplined in the Arab world — 'a happy, smiling country' is how his grandson, King Hussein, described his achievement. The Arab Legion was created, later to be commanded by Glubb Pasha, who made it into a force of worldwide renown. It was Glubb who first introduced bedouins into the armed forces — they were to earn legendary reputations during the Second World War.

In 1946 Transjordan was finally granted independence, and Emir Abdullah became king. Two years later Britain relinquished its mandate in Palestine and the state of Israel came into being, accompanied by bitter fighting between Jews and Arabs. 500,000 refugees flooded to Transjordan, putting severe strain on its already limited resources. In 1950, the West Bank of the Jordan — the part of Palestine that had remained in Arab hands — was

**Threshing and winnowing by traditional methods in Jordan.**

incorporated into the renamed Hashemite Kingdom of Jordan.

When King Abdullah was assassinated on 20 July 1951, his beloved eldest grandson, the fifteen-year-old Prince Hussein, was at his side. Just over a year later Hussein was King of Jordan, precipitated to the throne by the illness of his father, King Talal. Many of the years since 1952 have been turbulent. In the 1950s and 1960s the Arab world was swept by extremist nationalist sentiment which affected even the stability of Jordan. Attempts on King Hussein's life, and attempted coups, became almost commonplace for a while. Then came the Six Day War, in June 1967, when the West Bank was occupied by the Israelis, who have held it ever since; and yet more Palestinian refugees fled to Jordan.

Attempts to regain the occupied territories from Israel have provided one of the most troubled themes in the Arab world since 1967, and King Hussein himself has done all in his power to negotiate their restoration to their Arab inhabitants.

In a very real sense, Jordan today is the creation of King Hussein; with his encouragement education, medicine, welfare, the arts, agriculture, communications, banking and commerce have reached a high level of excellence and expertise in only a few decades, and this despite Jordan's lack of wealth compared with its oil-rich neighbours. Enlightened projects for the conservation of nature and natural resources are also being undertaken; and tourism is being developed to make Jordan's rich heritage accessible to more people. But the richest heritage of Hussein's kingdom lies in the Jordanian people, whose warmth, humour and spontaneous generosity, as well as their unfailing courtesy, illuminate and enrich any visitor's experience of this fascinating ancient and modern land.

None of this book would have been possible without the generosity of many people in Jordan.

My foremost thanks are to His Majesty King Hussein for graciously contributing such a warm and generous Foreword to this book; and to Her Majesty Queen Noor for her interest and encouragement in the publication of these aerial photographs.

HRH Prince Ra'ad bin Zeid has been an unfailing source of encouragement and wise advice, and my special thanks are due to him and to his wife, Princess Majda.

I am greatly indebted to HE Mr Zeid Rifai, the Prime Minister, and to HE Mr Marwan Kasim, Chief of the Royal Hashemite Court. Also to Mr Aktham Qusus, Director of the Prime Minister's Office. Without their support this book would not have seen the light of day.

To Mamdouh Bisharat and to his brother and sister-in-law, Suhail and Leila Bisharat, I owe a special debt of gratitude and affection; their hospitality, and their generosity in so many ways, have been boundless.

I have received generous and patient help from Khalid Shoman, Deputy Chairman of the Arab Bank, to whom, as to his wife Suha, I am deeply grateful.

My thanks are also due to Amar Khammash for sharing some of his valuable research on the villages of Jordan and their architecture.

I was given unstinting assistance by the Jordanian Ministry of Tourism, for which I am particularly grateful to its Director General, Nasri Atalla. With Ministry of Tourism vehicles and drivers, and the competent and charming guidance of Susan Nasir, I was taken to places that I might not otherwise have reached. It was they who initiated my contacts with the Royal Jordanian Air Force, and in particular with Major Younis Qudah, the Station Commander. The expert pilots of RJAF not only had a genius for setting up shots for me, but even gave the impression of enjoying this change from their normal routine almost as much as I was. To all of them my warmest thanks; also to Richard Ryan, who was so occupied in his efficient re-loading of my cameras that he hardly had time to look out of the helicopter.

It has been my special privilege to be able to see this glorious country from the air. From above, not only the contours of the earth can be seen, but also the whole layout of a city at a glance, its intersecting streets and outstanding buildings, and the geographical context in which it was built. With a building, or complex of buildings, the overall design of the architect is revealed in a way that is impossible to see so immediately from the ground. It is like an architectural site plan, but in three-dimensional colour, which helps to interpret the building when we look at it from ground level. It is my hope that with this book I can in some small way share the privilege I have had.

Jane Taylor
September 1988

# Amman

Nowhere in Jordan presents the changes of history so clearly as Amman, capital since 1921 of the Emirate of Transjordan, and since 1946 of the independent Hashemite Kingdom of Jordan.

As biblical Rabbah of the Ammonites, the city is first mentioned in Deuteronomy 3 as the place where the huge iron bedstead of Og King of Bashan had been taken — part of the spoils of an earlier war between the Bashanites and the Ammonites. Early in the sixth century BC Rabbah's doom at the hands of Nebuchadnezzar of Babylon was confidently prophesied first by Jeremiah (49:2) and then by Ezekiel (21:2 and 25:3-5); but these prophecies were unfulfilled, as Nebuchadnezzar destroyed Jerusalem instead.

In the Hellenistic period the city changed hands from time to time between the Syrian Seleucids and the Egyptian Ptolemies, and was rebuilt by Ptolemy II Philadelphus (283-246 BC) who renamed it Philadelphia after himself. The Nabataeans held it briefly, but Herod the Great drove them out around 30 BC. It was under the Romans that Philadelphia really began to prosper, as one of the ten cities of the Decapolis, and it was extensively rebuilt. It continued to flourish throughout the Byzantine period; also after the Arab conquest, for the ruins of a handsome eighth century Umayyad palace stand on top of the ancient Citadel (*below*).

Decline set in after the Abbasids transferred their capital from Damascus to Baghdad, and by the fifteenth century the city was abandoned and in ruins. So it remained until 1878 when the Ottomans established a settlement of Circassians here. But it remained small, even after the Hejaz railway was completed in 1905, improving its commercial position.

It was only after Emir Abdullah made Amman his capital in 1921 that it once again grew in size and prosperity, expanding from one steep hill to another in a creeping development of harmonious pale gold stone and white-painted concrete. It is today the seat of government, as well as the commercial, legal and administrative centre of Jordan.

# Amman

## The Roman Theatre

The most imposing monument from Roman Philadelphia is the theatre, originally set beside a small river and the main road through the city, known as the Decumanus Maximus. Built into the hillside of Jebel Jofeh, it accommodated an audience of 6000.

Jebel Jofeh became the main residential area for the affluent in the early years of the Emirate, but that distinction is now held by Jebel Amman. In 1948 the theatre and Roman tombs along the hillside here provided a first safe haven for some 50,000 Palestinian refugees fleeing from Israeli aggression. Within only two weeks, Amman's population was nearly doubled. Many decided to remain, gradually turning their tents into crowded permanent structures that stack almost one on top of another on the steep slopes. Few obtained a deed to their plots.

In 1980 the Urban Development Department (UDD), an agency for low-income housing, undertook to upgrade the area by assisting squatters to gain legal title through purchasing their plots and by providing water, sewers, drainage and footpaths. It also arranged loans to enable people to improve their homes further.

At the same time the UDD undertook programmes in health, education and vocational training. The health of infants and children is given priority throughout Jordan, and child mortality has fallen dramatically since 1948. In the years that the UDD has operated here, infant mortality has been reduced still further from 68 to under 40 per thousand. Immunization levels are high, and so is nutritional status, though family incomes are limited.

The UDD health workers are conducting routine house-to-house weighing and health discussions with the child's mother and other family members (*below*).

# Jerash

## Gerasa

One of the best preserved provincial Roman cities in the world, Jerash lies about 50 km north of Amman, in a fair and fertile valley in the heart of the hills of Gilead, with a stream running through the middle of it. Doubtless because of its abundant water supply, the area has been occupied since Neolithic times. In the Hellenistic period the city was known as Antioch on the Chrysorhoas (or Golden River, as the stream was grandly called); but nothing remains of this, nor of the brief Hasmonean occupation, for the glorious new Roman city of Gerasa obliterated everything of an earlier date. As one of the ten cities of the Decapolis, it entered on a long period of great prosperity.

In the first century AD a completely new town plan was drawn up in the classic Roman mould, with a main colonnaded street, or Cardo Maximus, on the north-south axis; two intersecting cross streets, the North and South Decumanus; and an encircling wall. At the south end of the Cardo is the highly unusual and very lovely Oval Piazza (*below*). Overlooking it is the second century Temple of Zeus, built on the site of several earlier temples; and beside this is the grander of the two theatres, with a seating capacity of over 3000. It is today used for the annual Jerash Festival. West of the Cardo, between the Piazza and the South Decumanus, a handsome building, only recently excavated, has been identified as the Agora, dating from the second century.

Dominating Jerash still is the great Temple of Artemis (*main photo, foreground*), dedicated to its patron goddess, set on a spacious terrace, or temenos, and approached from the Cardo through a monumental gate and stairway. North of this (*just out of view*) is the smaller north theatre and the North Decumanus.

In the Byzantine period many churches were built, and also a cathedral, utilizing Roman building material. Gerasa's heyday was already past when the Persians invaded in 614, and after the Arab conquest of 636 it continued as a minor town under the Umayyads, until shattered by the great earthquake of 747. A few years later the Caliphate transferred from Damascus to Baghdad, and the city faded into ruinous obscurity.

In 1806 a German scholar, Jasper Seetzen, rediscovered Gerasa, and was soon followed by an ever-increasing number of travellers. In 1878 the Ottomans settled a group of Circassians here; and their village grew into the modern town of Jerash.

# Ajlun

## Qala'at al-Rabadh

In the pine-clad hills just north of Jerash, towering above the village of Ajlun, stands a handsome fortress from which there is a splendid view westwards into the Jordan Valley. It looks like a Crusader castle, but it was built by the Arabs in 1184-85 as a defence against the expansionist Crusaders of the Latin Kingdom. It was built on the orders of the local governor, Azz al-Din Ausama, a cousin of the Ayyubid leader, Salah al-Din (Saladin), and is a superb example of Ayyubid military architecture. Two years after it was completed the fortress's original purpose had already been outlived, for Salah al-Din defeated the Crusaders at the battle of the Horns of Hattin, which marked the beginning of the end of their occupation of the Holy Land.

In 1214-15 Qala'at al-Rabadh was enlarged by Aybak ibn Abd Allah, major domo of the Caliph al-Muazzam; in 1260 it fell to the Mongols, but was later rebuilt by the Egyptian Mamluks. No longer needed for military purposes, it was used as an administrative centre responsible to Damascus.

Some of the stones with which the castle was built have crosses carved into them, giving credence to a tradition, recounted by a thirteenth century Arab historian that: 'an ancient monastery once stood on the site, inhabited by a Christian named Ajlun; when the monastery fell into ruin, the castle took its place and the name of the monk'.

*Below:* **Detail of the tower, Ajlun.**

# Umm Qeis

## Gadara

Little is known of the very early history of Gadara, a hilltop site in the north-western corner of Jordan with a magnificent view over the Yarmouk River, the Golan Heights and Lake Tiberias. Gadara is now chiefly known from the story (Matthew 8: 28-34) of Jesus casting out demons from two men and sending them into a herd of pigs which then rushed down the steep slope and drowned in the lake. The exact location of the miracle is unknown.

In the Hellenistic period, despite Gadara's reputation for impregnability, it changed hands like the rest of Jordan between the Ptolemies and the Seleucids, and it was captured by the Hasmonean ruler Alexander Jannaeus (103-76 BC). Little remains of the Hellenistic city; but some Nabataean finds indicate that they too were here briefly in the first century BC.

Gadara reached its full glory under the Romans as one of the Decapolis cities, and was especially noted for the richness of its intellectual life. It had flourishing schools of poetry and philosophy, of which the poet Meleager, born in Gadara in the first century BC, was the most distinguished son. The Gadarenes also revelled in the famous hot springs in the valley below; then, writes Strabo, they returned to 'the cooler heights of the city, solacing their leisure with plays performed in the theatres.'

There were two large theatres at Gadara, of which the smaller western one, dilapidated as it is, is the better preserved. It is built of black basalt and accommodated an audience of 3000. Still seated in the front row, as if petrified in mid-drama, is a headless white marble statue of Tyche (*below*), goddess of fortune and of the city. Beside the theatre stand the columns of an octagonal Byzantine church, built on the site of a Roman temple; and further west (*left of main photo*) is a baths complex, behind which, on the other side of what was once the main colonnaded street, the agora is currently being excavated.

Under the Byzantines, Gadara continued to flourish as the seat of a bishopric; but decline set in after the Arab conquest of 636. Its buildings have been cannibalized over the centuries, and a village of great charm grew up amongst the ruins. After archaeological work began in 1974, the villagers were moved into new housing nearby, and some of the handsome Arab houses are being restored alongside the excavation of the classical site.

# The Hills of

# Gilead

In the northern highlands of Jordan, near Umm Qeis, olives and sheep are the staple forms of agriculture. Throughout Jordan olives occupy a greater acreage than any other type of fruit-bearing tree. Wheat, as well as barley, animal fodder, legumes and some vegetables, is also grown in the highlands. Despite the increasing implementation of mechanized and modern cultivation methods, crop yields are still heavily dependent on highly erratic rainfall levels, making forward planning extremely difficult. In good years (25 inches/640 mm of rain) the yield is abundant; but it is drastically reduced in the many years of lower rainfall. Although Jordan is more than self-sufficient in fruit and vegetables, the production of dry grains (especially wheat) does not meet the country's needs and much has to be imported.

Sheep farming in Jordan has traditionally been largely in the hands of the bedouins, and also of settled farmers in areas of marginal rainfall. The ancient patterns are still observed — when the rains come in the autumn and winter, flocks are taken into the desert or deep wadis for the few months that they are clad with grass, to be brought to the better arable land in spring once the grain has been harvested. Jordan does not produce enough red meat for internal demand, and one of the government's agricultural development projects is the introduction of better breeds of sheep and cattle. It has already successfully increased the production and distribution of broiler chickens and dairy products.

By far the most productive agricultural area in Jordan is the Jordan Valley (Ghor), a 100km north-south rift lying below sea-level. Occupying less than 1% of the total area of Jordan, it produces 40% of its agricultural output. Extensive and increasingly efficient irrigation has been provided through the East Ghor Canal Project and the building of dams, thus overcoming the problem of minimal rainfall (2-8 inches/50-200 mm per annum). Citrus fruit and vegetables are the main production, and there has recently been an extension of wheat growing in the valley, using the winter season, to try to reduce Jordan's dependence on imported wheat.

*Below:* **Bedouin boy holding a lamb.**

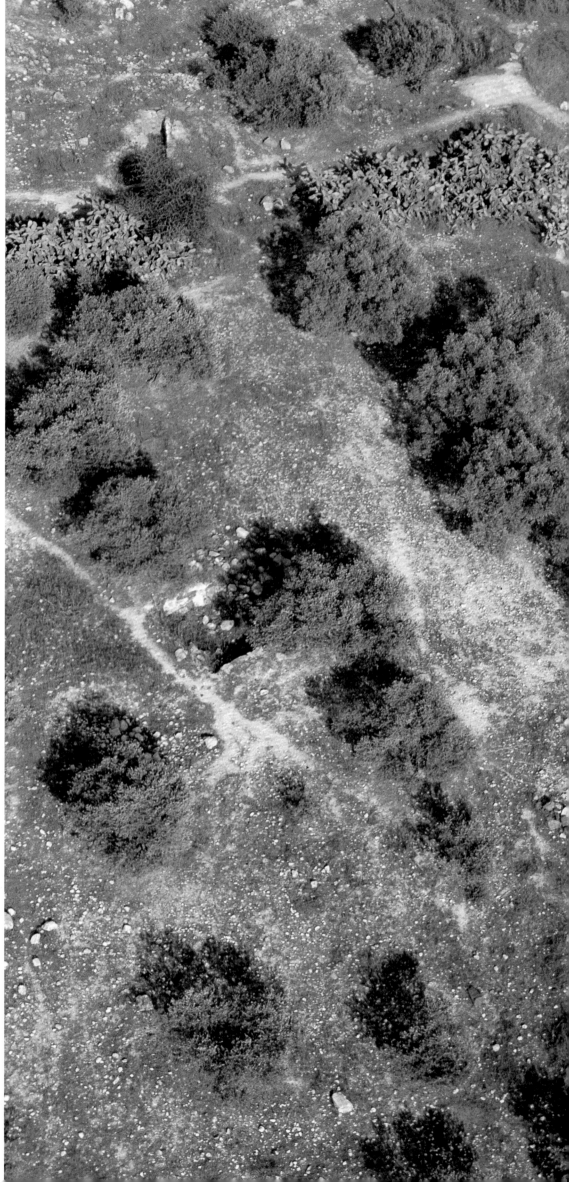

# Tabaqat Fahl

## Pella

Magnificently set in a fold of the hills that rise from the Jordan Valley, Pella is one of the most ancient sites in Jordan. It is perfectly situated, for there is a spring here which issues into a small river and never runs dry. The tell itself seems to have been continuously occupied since Neolithic times for some flints from this period have been found there; and some recent finds 2km north of the tell even date to Palaeolithic times, around 100,000 years ago. Several artefacts from the Chalcolithic period, around the fourth millennium BC, have been found on the tell; and there are more remains from the Bronze and Iron Ages. Excavations by a team of Australian archaeologists have revealed much in the decade they have been working here, but still more remains hidden.

The first literary reference to the city is from the nineteenth century BC when it is mentioned in Egyptian texts as Pihilum, or Pehel. It was a flourishing trade centre, with links with Syria and Cyprus as well as Egypt. There is, however, no mention of it in the Bible.

On the division of Alexander's Empire, its name was changed to Pella — either in honour of Alexander's birthplace, or as a Hellenization of Pihilum, or both. It changed hands between the Ptolemies and Seleucids, and was sacked by the Hasmonean Alexander Jannaeus. After Pompey's conquest in 63 BC its prosperity increased further as one of the cities of the Roman Decapolis, and the Roman city — including a theatre built in a curve of the hillside — more or less eliminated the Hellenistic city. Under the Byzantines there was yet more building, in particular of churches — on the hillside overlooking the valley stands one such church (*below, and foreground of main photo*), while another is near the river at the foot of the ancient tell.

After the seventh century Arab conquest, Pella continued as an Umayyad city for just over 100 years, and some superb pottery remains have been found here, made in the Jerash kilns. But like so many places in Jordan, the city was destroyed by the terrible earthquake of 747. The site continued to be occupied during the Abbasid and Mamluk periods, but it was now a much smaller and more rural community. There was still a mud-brick village on the tell until 1970, but it was bombed in an Israeli strike across the border.

# Umm al-Jimal

The extensive black basalt city of Umm al-Jimal lies like a dark encrustation on the flat desert of northern Jordan. So many of the buildings still stand to two, or even three, storeys that it seems as if its abandonment must have been within living memory — in fact it has been deserted for about 1200 years.

The Nabataeans established a settlement here in the first century BC during their northerly expansion, perhaps as a staging-post on the trade route between Damascus and the south. As there are no springs or wells, the entire water supply had to be collected during the rainy season in hundreds of cisterns.

Herod the Great drove the Nabataeans out of their northern domains around 30 BC, and the Romans soon extended their rule over the entire area. Umm al-Jimal was greatly enlarged from the second century AD onwards, and became an important military base — it was enclosed within walls; a new reservoir was built (*left of main photo*), as well as a sophisticated hydraulic system outside the city to supply its cisterns and reservoirs; and a vast, but now ruinous, fort was constructed (*left of the reservoir*) — to be replaced under the Byzantines in the early fifth century by the much smaller, and well preserved, barracks (*centre of main photo*), for by now the military role of the city had diminished.

Under the Byzantines Umm al-Jimal continued to grow — many houses were built, fourteen churches and a cathedral (*standing isolated below the barracks*). It also flourished under the Umayyads — still with a Christian community — but earthquakes, especially that of 747, caused considerable damage; and the Abbasid removal to Baghdad ensured that the city was never rebuilt. It remained abandoned until the early twentieth century, when some Druzes from the nearby Jebel al-Druze took up brief residence here.

*Below:* The Roman barracks seen through the arches of the West Church.

# Azraq Oasis

The oasis of Azraq, 80 km east of Amman, lies in a vast shallow basin where the black basalt desert meets the head of the Wadi Sirhan, which stretches south-east into Saudi Arabia. Millions of years ago it was covered by sea; a mere one million years ago there was a vast lake here; then fertile plains brimming with animals and birds. Today it is desert, with an oasis of swamps and pools and palm trees at its heart.

Until recently Azraq was astonishingly rich in migrant birds of every kind, *en route* between Europe and Africa — now both swamps and birds have diminished dramatically as water is being pumped in vast quantities to supply Amman. The Jordanian Royal Society for the Conservation of Nature has created the Azraq Wetlands Reserve and is working to redeem the situation; it also established the nearby Shaumari Wildlife Reserve in 1967, the first in Jordan, whose greatest success so far has been the reintroduction of the Arabian Oryx into its natural habitat.

Azraq's abundant water attracted the Romans who, possibly under Septimius Severus (AD 193-211), established here the eastern military outpost of their Province of Arabia. In the basalt castle (*centre of main photo*) an inscription was found dedicating it to the Emperors Diocletian and Maximian, probably around AD 300. Roman doorways — like those of the main entrance (*below*) — still turn on pivots made in one piece with the door itself, which fit into sockets cut into the threshold and lintel. Azraq continued as a military outpost under the Byzantines.

The Umayyad Caliphs of the seventh to eighth centuries, enthusiastic hunters as they were, used the fortress for their expeditions in pursuit of the thronging wildlife in and around the marshes. It must have been neglected after the Abbasid removal to Baghdad, for in the early thirteenth century the Ayyubid governor, Azz al-Din Aybak, rebuilt it — again for military purposes — recording his work in an Arabic inscription above the main doorway. The Ottomans also established a garrison here after their conquest in 1516.

Azraq's most recent military use was in the Arab Revolt when T.E. Lawrence made the castle his headquarters in the winter of 1917/18, and from here prepared the great assault on Damascus — 'Azraq the remote,' he called the place, a 'luminous silky Eden'.

# Qasr al-Tuba

In 1896 a Czech Arabist, Alois Musil, was told by bedouins of some wonderful old palaces deep in the desert, decorated with columns and paintings and inscriptions. Two years later he found Qasr al-Tuba, the most southerly and remote of a group of castles built by the Umayyad caliphs of Damascus in the first half of the eighth century. Bedouin in their origin, these caliphs escaped at every opportunity from the city to the unconfining desert where they could hawk and hunt and race their Arab horses.

But the city had already left its mark on them, and while at first they may have camped in the desert in black tents, they soon built a scattering of palaces made beautiful with arches and columns, frescoes and carvings, and luxurious with heated baths, spacious courtyards and great halls for music and dancing. They are enchanting examples of early Islamic architecture.

Qasr al-Tuba, the largest of the Umayyad palaces of Jordan, has been dated to 743-4, when the dissolute Walid II was caliph. It consists of two symmetrical and matching enclosures, side by side, forming almost a double square. Only the buildings of the north corner are still nearly intact, and most of the lower part of the western wall; but the outline of the rest of the complex — which was probably never completed — is clear from the air (*main photo*). The walls are of three courses of stone, above which they are built of sun-dried mud bricks, as are the barrel-vaulted roofs. Stone was also used to frame the door arches (*below*); and Musil found some finely carved stone door jambs and lintels — but these have long since disappeared.

# Qasr Amra

A few days after his discovery of Qasr al-Tuba, Alois Musil found an even more spectacular desert palace — Qasr Amra, a harmonious little stone-built complex in Wadi Butm, named after the butm, or terebinth, trees which grow here. Inside he found the walls covered with vivid frescoes, parts of which — considering their neglect for so many centuries, the smoke from bedouin fires, and human graffiti — are still in passably good condition.

It is thought that this little cluster of buildings may be all that is left of a larger complex, which perhaps included a fortress and living quarters. Today there is an audience hall of three parallel barrel-vaults, with an alcove and two small rooms off it; and a bath house of three rooms, including a calidarium covered with a dome, and with under-floor hypocaust heating. It is thought to have been built by the Caliph Walid I around 711.

The frescoes are of exceptional interest, not only for their joyous naturalism, but for their very existence — although the Koran itself does not prohibit painting, the later *Traditions* do. The first iconoclast edict was by Caliph Yazid II (720-24), ordering all human images to be destroyed. Happily these frescoes escaped. Here, in those pre-iconoclast times, the artists were uninhibited in their depictions of human life — hunting scenes; the goddesses of Poetry, Philosophy and History; musicians, dancers, and women and children bathers, all in varying states of *déshabillé*; and four figures of the enemies of Islam conquered by Walid I — the Byzantine Emperor, the Visigoth King of Spain, the Sassanian Emperor and the Negus of Abyssinia.

Perhaps the most remarkable fresco is that in the little dome of the calidarium (*below*), for it is a very early representation of the night sky in the round instead of on a flat surface. The Great Bear, the Little Bear, Andromeda, Cassiopeia and Orion are still distinguishable — but the artist seems to have been copying from a drawing which he has transposed in mirror-image, reversing the relationships of all the constellations.

# Qasr al-Kharaneh

The only one of the Umayyad desert castles which looks as if it were built with defence in mind is Qasr al-Kharaneh, though this may be more apparent than real. It is constructed of large, undressed stones, with smaller stones laid in rows between them. The exterior was originally completely plastered, emphasising its solid appearance. Its uncompromising squareness is broken by a round tower at each corner and a semi-circular one in the middle of each wall, except on the south side where the sole entrance occupies the centre. The arrow-slits may have been for ventilation rather than defence. Set on the path of several ancient trade routes, it was probably used as a caravanserai.

Inside, it is divided into two storeys with a small open courtyard in the centre. Stables for the animals are to the left and right just inside the gate, while accommodation for human beings is around the three other sides of the courtyard and on the upper floor. In one of the upper rooms a painted Kufic inscription over the door bears the date 711, in the time of Caliph Walid I; but there is some doubt whether this refers to the original construction or a later rebuilding. One of the features of Qasr al-Kharaneh is the considerable use of arches and vaults in every room, some of them with semi-domes, and the arches in many cases spring from groups of three engaged columns (*below*). All the rooms were plastered and often carved with decorative patterns.

# Qasr al-Mushatta

The most richly decorated of the Umayyad palaces in Jordan was Qasr al-Mushatta, now near the Queen Alia International Airport just south of Amman. Stone carvings of great delicacy and vitality once adorned it, but today only a few pieces still in place bear witness to its original glory, for the Ottoman Sultan Abdul Hamit II gave them to Kaiser Wilhelm II in 1903, and shortly afterwards they were stripped off and shipped to Germany. They can now be seen in the Pergamum Museum in East Berlin.

Qasr al-Mushatta is a great square walled enclosure with round towers at the corners, and five semi-circular ones at regular intervals in each side, except on the south, whose centre is occupied by the gateway. It was around this gateway that the magnificent carvings were originally situated, standing to a considerable height, and adorned with vine and flower tracery, and large rosettes, within a great band of linked upright and inverted triangles.

Inside, the two outer sections are virtually untouched, for the palace was never completed. In the centre, a complex of buildings just inside the entrance led into a spacious central court, beyond which was the royal audience hall and residence – possibly for Walid II, the same caliph who built Qasr al-Tuba, for this palace too is believed to date from 743-4. The audience hall is fascinating – basilical as you enter from the court, with a trefoil apse which was originally covered by a great dome. On either side of it the buildings were covered with barrel vaults, some of which remain. The whole of this part of the palace is constructed on the inside with burnt mud bricks.

*Below:* **Detail of stone carving, Qasr al-Mushatta.**

# Madaba

The rambling modern appearance of Madaba, a mainly Christian town 33 km south of Amman, belies the fact that it is the site of a very ancient settlement which occupied an artificial mound, or tell, rising above the surrounding tableland. Mentioned in the Bible as Medeba at the time of the Exodus (Numbers: 21,30; Joshua 13:9), it was then an Amorite town close to the Moab border, and it changed hands frequently. It was named in the famous Mesha stele, or Moabite stone, which recorded the achievements of Mesha, King of Moab in the mid-ninth century BC — one of which was to regain Madaba from the Israelites. In the Hellenistic period, and under the Romans, it was a flourishing provincial town with temples and colonnaded streets and surrounded by a strong wall.

Under the Byzantines Madaba became the seat of a bishopric, and in 451 its bishop attended the Council of Chalcedon. During this period, and particularly in the sixth century, mosaics were lavished on churches and public and private buildings. Most famous is the wonderful, if fragmentary, map of Palestine and Jordan in the Greek Orthodox Church of St George (*left of main photo*). It includes a fascinating plan of Jerusalem (*below*): on the left is the north gate from which two colonnaded streets run south. On the straight street through the heart of the city stands the domed Holy Sepulchre. Clearly inscribed above the north and east gates is the legend 'Holy city of Jerusa[lem]'.

Madaba was sacked by the Persians in AD 614, and its ruin was completed by the earthquake of 747. It stood abandoned for over 1000 years until, around 1880, a group of about 2000 Christians from Kerak (*see page 62*) settled here. It was they, in the process of rebuilding, who found the mosaics buried under the rubble.

# Mount Nebo

Mount Nebo, in the hills of Moab, is the place from which Moses looked out over the land of Canaan which God had forbidden him to enter; and here he died and was buried (Deuteronomy 32,49; 34,1-6). On a clear day there is a magnificent panoramic view over the Dead Sea to the Judaean hills, and as far as Jerusalem.

Around AD 394, an intrepid Roman lady called Egeria visited Mount Nebo in the course of an extensive Christian pilgrimage through the Byzantine Empire. She struggled to the top of the hill mostly on a donkey, but scrambling up the steeper parts on foot. At the summit she found a 'small church' cared for by some 'holy men' who assured her that Moses was buried there, for this was the tradition that had been handed down by their ancestors who had always lived there. Less than one hundred years later another pilgrim, Peter the Iberian, wrote of a 'very large church' with 'many monasteries' around it; but archaeological evidence points to it being the same church that Egeria saw, the difference in size merely a matter of vision. Later the site was abandoned.

Excavations at Siyagha on the highest ridge of Mount Nebo (*main photograph*), have revealed a cluster of monastic buildings around a sixth century basilica church. Within the church are the remains of an earlier chapel (perhaps that seen by Egeria and Peter), and a second or third century AD structure, the earliest on the site, which may have been a mausoleum. Since 1976 several mosaics have been found, including a magnificent and very large pavement with vivid representations of people and animals.

The hills in this region are rocky and arid, with patches of soil between the rocks for which modern agricultural equipment is useless. Ploughing with donkeys (*below*) is the only way of utilizing what little soil there is.

# Machaerus

Known today as Mukawir, this dramatic hilltop is the traditional site of the execution of John the Baptist.

A fortress was first built here by the Hasmonean ruler Alexander Jannaeus (103-76 BC) to defend Perea against the expansionist Nabataeans. His widow Alexandra, confident of the site's inviolability, stored her treasure here — to no avail, as the Romans destroyed it in 63 BC. It was restored by Herod the Great (37-4 BC) who, according to the contemporary historian Josephus, 'built a wall round the very summit and erected towers at the corners, each 90 feet high. In the middle of this enclosure he built a palace, breath-taking in size and beauty.'

When Herod's son, Herod Antipas, divorced his Nabataean wife to marry Herodias, his brother Philip's wife, John the Baptist outspokenly condemned his behaviour. It was at Machaerus, it is said, that John was imprisoned, and Herodias' daughter Salome danced and demanded the Baptist's head on a charger. During the Judaean war many refugees fled from Jerusalem to Machaerus for safety. It was finally destroyed, again by the Romans, in AD 72.

In the wild and beautiful mountains that surround Machaerus live the Bani Hamida bedouins, until recently nomadic, but now settled in a handful of little villages. Lovely as the area is, and despite government provision of a road, running water, schools, clinics and post offices, it is bleak and poor, and many of the men have had to leave home to seek work elsewhere.

In 1985 Save the Children initiated an imaginative project to develop the main traditional craft of the bedu women — rug-weaving (*below*) — and thus to provide a new and vital source of additional income. Using the age-old flat hand-looms, three hundred women now weave for the project, being provided with wool and given the profit from the sale of their rugs. Their traditional designs are now being used with modern and more subtle colour combinations — the results are very beautiful and much in demand, many being sold abroad. The extra money that the women earn is spent on better food, education for their children, and home improvements. It is a magnificent success.

# Petra, the 'Rock'

The ancient city of Petra lies in the dramatic barrier of russet-coloured mountains that run beside the rift valley of Wadi Arabah from the Dead Sea to the Gulf of Aqaba. 'Rock' is what Petra means, echoing its biblical name of Selah; and these wild and weirdly-shaped rocks which surround it seem at first sight so impenetrable that it is hardly surprising that for over 1000 years the city was lost in obscurity, known only to the bedouin.

Possibly as early as 580 BC the Nabataeans, nomads from Arabia, began filtering into these mountains, filling the gap left by the Edomites who had moved into the richer, more fertile lands to the west of Wadi Arabah, which lay almost deserted after King Nebuchadnezzar had taken the Jews to captivity in Babylon.

Nomads though they were, the Nabataeans showed a prodigious aptitude for trade. All the major trade routes of the day converged in their new territory, and it was near that point that they made their capital in Wadi Mousa, a valley blessed with abundant water and natural defences. From here they took over and controlled the caravan routes — to their enormous profit.

They also developed an astonishingly harmonious architecture which, while borrowing ideas from other cultures, remained wholly Nabataean. A very early borrowing was the Assyrian crow-step design (*below*), used here to decorate tomb façades. Petra may appear as a vast city of the dead; it was an even vaster city of the living in its time, but the buildings for the living proved less durable than the carved tombs for the dead.

Only a fraction of ancient Petra has as yet been uncovered, and many mysteries remain unsolved, one of them over the so-called 'djin' blocks (*bottom centre of main photograph*) of which there are some 25 — perhaps early tombs, perhaps representations of the god Dusares. This group of three is near the entrance to the Siq, the mile-long cleft in the mountain (*diagonal shadow, left of main photograph*) that leads into the city.

Passionate in the defence of their freedom, and for long possessing the wealth and the diplomatic skills to maintain it, the Nabataeans remained independent long after the other peoples of Jordan and Palestine had submitted, first to the heirs of Alexander, then to Rome. It was not until AD 106 that the Nabataean kingdom was taken over by the Romans and became their Province of Arabia.

Try as the Romans did to improve matters, Petra's economy and culture were by now in decline, and a remote survival became the order of the day. It survived the Byzantine period, when it gained new distinction as the seat of a bishopric, later raised to metropolitan status. Even after the Arab conquest of 636 it kept a certain eminence because it was on the caliphs' pilgrimage route from Damascus to Mecca. But with the earthquake of 747, and the transfer of the caliphate to Baghdad soon after, the story of ancient Petra comes to an end.

# The Rediscovery of Petra

On 22 August 1812 a young Swiss explorer wrote in his journal, 'I was particularly desirous of visiting Wadi Mousa, of the antiquities of which I had heard the country people speak in terms of great admiration... I therefore pretended to have made a vow to slaughter a goat in honour of Haroun (Aaron), whose tomb I knew was situated at the extremity of the valley, and by this stratagem I thought I should have the means of seeing the valley in my way to the tomb.'

Thus did John Burckhardt — under the remarkably convincing alias of Ibrahim ibn Abdallah, a devout Muslim — discover Petra, known to the west only from a few tantalizing references by some classical authors. With a reluctant guide and a sacrificial goat, Burckhardt set out for Wadi Mousa; if his cover had been blown, and his journal found, he would undoubtedly have been killed.

Passing through the towering narrow defile of the Siq, Burkhardt emerged face-to-face with the glowing perfection of the Treasury (*below and main photo*), carved out of the solid rock. It is justly the most famous monument in Petra, the loveliest and least eroded; but it is certainly not a treasury, probably either a tomb or a temple, created to impress all who entered the Nabataean capital. As with everything in Petra, its original name, like its original purpose, is unknown. Burckhardt was told it was called Khasneh al-Faroun, Pharaoh's Treasury, and so it is still known today — from the superstition that treasure had been hidden in the urn at the top by the most powerful of all black magicians, generally identified with some mythical Pharaoh.

Even the date when the Treasury was carved is unknown; perhaps it was in the time of King Aretas III Philhellene (84-56 BC), when the Nabataeans were at the height of their expansion, and of their exposure to Hellenistic ideas and architecture — here brilliantly transformed into a design that is still distinctively Nabataean. It was to exert a powerful influence over later works.

The theatre (*centre background of main photograph*) dates from about the first century AD. Its 33 rows of seats, seating up to 4000 people, were carved out of the solid rock of the hillside.

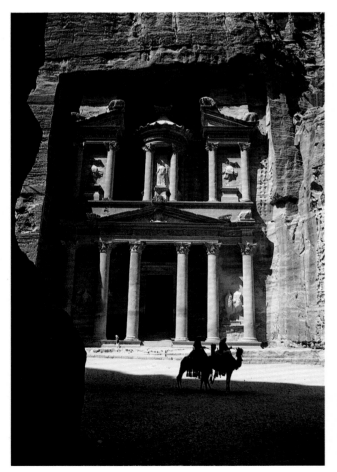

# The Rose-red City

*'It seems no work of Man's creative hand,*
*By labour wrought as wavering fancy planned;*
*But from the rock as if by magic grown,*
*Eternal, silent, beautiful, alone!...*
*Match me such a marvel save in Eastern clime,*
*A rose-red city half as old as Time.'*
from *Petra*, by Dean Burgon

When his Journals were published in 1822, John Burckhardt had been dead for five years, struck down by dysentery in Cairo at the age of 32. News of his discovery had already reached Europe, and now tourists came in ever increasing numbers to see Petra for themselves, mystifying the bedouin with their enthusiasm to measure, map, write, draw, paint and clamber up and down rocks.

The first were two Royal Navy commanders, the Hon. C.L. Irby and Mr J. Mangles, who came nervously and briefly in 1818, unconvincingly disguised in what they thought was Arab dress. The Marquis de Laborde followed in 1826, also dressed *à l'Arabe*, and produced some wonderfully romantic etchings. Probably the finest artist to visit Petra was the Royal Academician David Roberts in 1839; and Edward Lear too made some hauntingly lovely drawings.

Apart from the astonishing architecture, it was the colours that captivated people — even if they had never been there, like Dean Burgon when he wrote his famous poem. When he did visit a few years later he confessed in a letter to his sister that 'there is nothing rosy about Petra, not by any means.'

Edward Lear's Italian cook was nearer the mark when he exclaimed, 'Oh, Signore, we have come into a world where everything is made of chocolate, ham, curry-powder and salmon.' Perhaps he had missed the purple, grey, deep red and cream striations that also occur so vividly in the rock (*below*).

In the Outer Siq a lovely group of tombs combines the earlier crow-step design with Hellenistic doors and pilasters. Further on, in the eastern cliff overlooking the centre of the city, a later group (*main photo*), known as the Royal Tombs, shows a stronger classical influence and an increased enthusiasm for sheer size. Most monumental of all is the Palace Tomb (*far left*), named after its supposed resemblance to a Roman palace. To its right is the Corinthian tomb, a rather unsatisfactory crib from the magnificent Treasury, and more eroded.

# The High Places of Petra

At the top of one of the hills overlooking Petra stands the Deir (*opposite*) a magnificent façade influenced by the design of the Treasury, but larger and more simply adorned. It must have been carved late in the Nabataean period, and could have been either a temple or a tomb. A processional way leads up long, steep paths and great flights of steps until it opens into a wide terrace, dominated by this monument, whose size dwarfs mere mortals. The grand ascent, the vast scale of the Deir itself, and the great terrace, all indicate a place of special sacredness; here huge congregations could take part in religious rituals and festivals. Its name –

meaning monastery – is something of a misnomer; but it was converted to Christian use in the fifth century, for there are crosses carved on the walls of the inner chamber.

On another ridge above Petra, also reached by a grand processional way, are two small plateaux, separated by a gully, which together formed the main religious centre of the ancient Nabataeans. On one plateau stand two obelisks (*above*), about 20 feet (6 m) high and about 100 feet (30 m) apart. To create them the Nabataeans had to cut away the whole of the mountain top – a labour almost certainly only undertaken in the service of their greatest

deities, the god Dusares and goddess Al Uzza, who were in earliest times represented as solid blocks of stone.

On the second plateau, a large area was cut level as the Nabataeans' High Place of Sacrifice, with a low offerings table in the midst of an open court, and a high altar raised above it at one end. Here ritual blood sacrifices (probably only animals) were made to Dusares and Al Uzza, looking out – as does the place of the obelisks – over a spectacular view, with Petra itself in the valley below, and around it the limitless mountains.

# A Bedouin Encampment

'I am black, but comely, O daughters of Jerusalem, like the tents of Kedar.'

The black goat hair tent – *al-beit al-sha'ar*, or house of hair to the bedouin who live in it – already had a long history when King Solomon extolled its comeliness. For thousands of years, as the nomadic bedu moved throughout the length and breadth of the Arabian deserts in search of water and pasture for their camels and goats, these portable houses of hair have provided shelter from sun and rain, a permanent home and sanctuary in their endless wanderings.

The life of the bedu in Jordan today – only seven per cent of the population – has changed dramatically in recent years, influenced by the perceived benefits offered by modern society. Most have settled into small villages, and cultivation has to a large extent replaced herding. But still in the spring many bedu leave their villages and take their tents to seek pasture for their flocks, returning to their villages for the winter.

Near Petra there are two bedouin groups – the Bdoul, who now live permanently in a village built for them by the government; and the Amareen, who have remained largely nomadic. The main photo shows a family of Amareen encamped among rocks with holes cut into them by the ancient inhabitants of the land. A long narrow strip of black goat hair tent-cloth can be seen, in the process of being woven; and small patches of land have been tilled and planted with winter wheat (it was October).

One of the most important tasks for the women is the daily making of the large thin circles of unleavened bread, or *shrak*. Nowadays the flour is often bought ready milled, then kneaded with water and a little salt to the right consistency (*below*). All vessels used to be of wood, but today aluminium and plastic prevail. Pieces of dough are broken off and rounded into small cakes, later to be expertly patted and tossed between flat palmed hands until it forms a large paper-thin circle, which is then thrown onto a convex iron baking-tray set on three stones over a fire. Turned over once, it is ready in a few seconds.

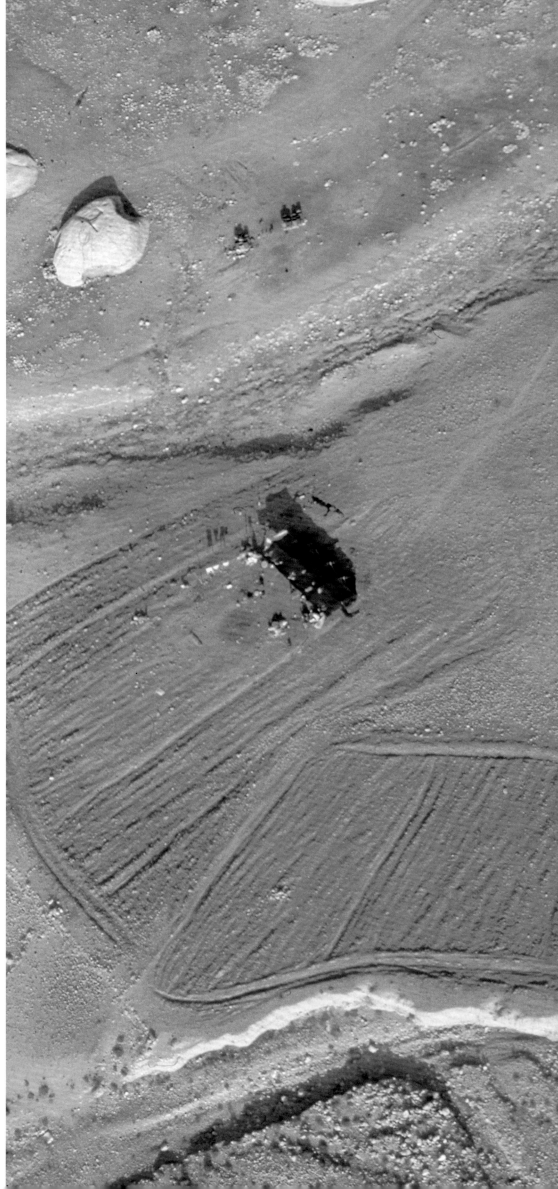

# Wadi Rum

'They were not unbroken walls of rock, but were built sectionally, in crags like gigantic buildings along the two sides of their street. Deep alleys, fifty feet across, divided the crags, whose plans were smoothed by the weather into huge apses and bays, and enriched with surface fretting and fracture, like design... They gave the finishing semblance of Byzantine architecture to this irresistible place: this processional way greater than imagination... Landscapes, in childhood's dream, were so vast and silent.' (T.E. Lawrence: *The Seven Pillars of Wisdom*)

Throughout the Arab Revolt, Lawrence would return to Wadi Rum, either in person or in imagination, when in need of solace, finding that 'Rumm's glory would not let a man waste himself in feverish regrets.' Appropriately, a significant part of David Lean's epic, *Lawrence of Arabia*, was filmed here.

Wadi Rum has been inhabited since earliest times, and seems to have been an important centre for the Nabataeans, for the ruins of a Nabataean temple have been found at the foot of the great massif of Jebel Rum.

There is a small fort here, one of a string built in 1933 by Glubb Pasha, as an outpost of the Desert Patrol — now known as the Bedouin Police (*below*) — which he had created only three years earlier. The bedu who joined it were transformed into an unflinching and disciplined force that represented everything that was most formidable and romantic in Middle East warfare. They won legendary reputations in the Second World War. Glubb himself designed their uniform — long khaki skirt, red sash, lanyard and bullet bandolier, a silver dagger tucked into the belt, and on the head a red-chequered *shamagh* held in place by a black *aghal*. They were the cynosure of every eye.

The Bedouin Police are still a formidable force, though now mostly mechanized rather than on camels. They patrol the borders to combat smuggling, in particular of arms and drugs; but much of their work is concerned with local security and social welfare, working in collaboration with the Ministries of Education and Health to maintain services in remote areas. The base at Wadi Rum is now largely a sideshow for the benefit of tourists.

# Aqaba

Jordan's only seaport, Aqaba, lies half encircled by mountains at the head of the Gulf of Aqaba, an arm of the Red Sea. The earliest settlement so far discovered here dates to about 3500 BC and includes smelting furnaces for the copper mined in Wadi Arabah. It was part of Edom at the time of the Exodus, and the towns of Elath/Eloth and Ezion-Geber are mentioned in the Bible. The Edomites also smelted copper here; and King Solomon later built a fleet at Ezion Geber to export copper to Ophir.

It continued as a flourishing port and trading centre, and was controlled successively by the Nabataeans, the Ptolemies (who called it Berenice) and the Romans who established a military base here at the end of Trajan's great paved road from Damascus. They called it Ailana.

Under the Byzantines it became the seat of a bishopric, and in 630 Bishop Yuhanna ibn Ru'ba made a peace treaty with the Prophet Muhammad on behalf of the people of Aqaba. Under the Arabs the city was known as Ayla, and the tenth century geographer Muqaddasi wrote that it was 'great in prosperity with its palms and fish; it is the port of Palestine and the storehouse of the Hejaz.' This medieval walled town is now being excavated. The Crusaders, under Baldwin I of Jerusalem, captured Ayla in 1116. Later it was taken by Salah al-Din, regained by Renaud de Chatillon, lord of Kerak, before being finally won back by the Arabs. It was during the thirteenth century that its name became Aqaba.

To the south of the modern town of Aqaba, near the shore, stands a medieval fortress (*below*) whose original may have been built by the Crusaders, but all inscriptions are in Arabic and record building work around 1320 and 1505. Thereafter its main use was as a fortified caravanserai for Egyptian pilgrims en route to Mecca.

Under the Ottomans Aqaba dwindled into a poor place, attached to the province of the Hejaz, and its significance was further eroded when the Suez Canal was completed in 1869, and shipping took over the pilgrim trade. When Alois Musil visited it in 1910 he wrote of extensive plantations of date palms, and said there were 'about thirty huts, inhabited by nineteen families... the majority of the inhabitants are the descendants of Egyptian soldiers and pilgrims who fell ill at al-Akaba, were cured, and married there.'

In 1917 the capture of Aqaba (in which T.E. Lawrence played an important part) was a turning point in the Arab Revolt, and it became for a time the headquarters of Emir Feisal. The Hashemite coat of arms above the entrance to the fort dates from this time. Only in 1925, four years after the establishment of the Emirate of Transjordan, was Aqaba officially detached from the Hejaz and incorporated into Transjordan.

Aqaba is today Jordan's fastest growing city. As the only port, it has been greatly developed for import and export by sea. The major export is that of phosphates. Besides this, Aqaba is being developed as a tourist resort, particularly agreeable in autumn, winter and spring, offering not only water sports, but also snorkelling and scuba diving to see the beautiful coral reefs with their colourful plants and fish.

# Shobak
## Crusader Castle

Just off the King's Highway a short distance north of Petra stands an impressive Crusader castle, crowning a cone of rock which rises above a wild and rugged landscape dotted with green valleys. It is today known as Shobak, but to the Crusaders it was Crak de Montréal or Mons Regalis, the fortress of the royal mount. It was built in 1115 by King Baldwin I of Jerusalem to guard the road from Damascus to Egypt, and was the first of a string of similar strongholds in the Latin Kingdom of Jerusalem.

Salah al-Din attacked it on several occasions, finally capturing it in 1189 when the Crusaders were losing their foothold throughout the Holy Land. It passed to the Mamluks in 1260 and they restored it in the following century, adorning its walls and towers with Arabic inscriptions which testify to their work. Since then it has lain largely untouched, gradually falling into greater disrepair.

The walls and towers are still reasonably intact, but inside the castle consists mainly of tumbled stones with a few walls and arches. One of the most fascinating remains is the ancient well-shaft cut deep into the rock, with 375 steps leading down to the water supply at the bottom.

There are several small villages in the area, for there are abundant springs and fertile valleys where olives, grapes, figs, and apricots are grown, as well as grain crops. Earlier this century the castle itself was occupied by a few local families, and there was a market within its walls which served all the villages. Before 1948 trade links were mainly with Palestine, and the villagers would make regular trips to Beersheba to sell livestock and ghee (camel butter), and to Hebron and Jerusalem to buy sugar, oranges and cloth. Today they have to go to Maan.

# Dana

The little village of Dana perches on a shelf in the hillside that drops down into the great rift valley of Wadi Arabah.

The one approach road comes to an end at the beginning of the village; thereafter narrow paths, just wide enough to walk in, run between the flat-roofed houses. Built of stone and wood, and plastered with mud, they blend perfectly with the landscape, not only in colour and texture, but also in the way in which the contours of the land are reflected in the levels of the roofs.

The site was almost certainly occupied in ancient times, built beside the spring whose abundant water irrigated the carefully-made terraces on the hillside, on which grow a variety of fruit and vegetables.

Dana is a fascinating village, unique in Jordan, its remoteness having ensured its freedom from incongruous development. Here we can see the typical nuclear growth of the *fellahin* (settled farmer) village where, as families grew and married, new dwellings were built on to the original home, with shared roofs so that communications were at least as often at roof level as at ground level. The roof is a very important part of the house, not only for visiting neighbours, but for sleeping on in summer, and for drying hay and fruits. It is the main point of entry of foodstuffs into the house, as the single door is too narrow to admit bulky items. Ramps enable hay and grain to be taken up to the roof from where they are let down through holes into storage silos inside the house.

The architecture is a fascinating reflection of the materials available. The single rectangular unit is divided by arches at intervals of 1½–2 metres – the average length of the wooden roof poles made from local trees. It is a style that has been used for centuries – the domestic part of ancient Petra must have looked very like Dana today.

It is, however, a dying village. Most of the houses have been abandoned, the families having moved in pursuit of easier transport and modern facilities to a new village further up the hillside near the main road. Plans by the Ministry of Tourism to preserve Dana have been thwarted by lack of money.

Not far from the village, the Royal Society for the Conservation of Nature is establishing the new Dana Wildlife Reserve to protect the magnificent scenery of this area, to preserve its unique grove of 2–3000-year-old cypress trees as well as the oak, pine and pistachio forests, and to reinforce the residual populations of mountain gazelle, ibex and striped hyena that were once abundant here.

# Kerak

## Crusader Castle

The magnificent Crusader fortress of Kerak — Crak des Moabites, or Le Pierre du Désert to the Crusaders — soars above its valleys and hills like a great ship riding waves of rock. But Kerak's origins go back long before the Crusaders; the earliest remains are Iron Age, shortly after the Exodus, when this was a part of Moab. It was known as Kir-haraseth, and its doom was prophesied by Isaiah (16:7), who mentions its 'raisin-cakes', presumably a local speciality. Then it falls out of history until the Byzantine period, when it was important enough to have an archbishop.

It was the Crusaders who made Kerak famous. The fortress was built in 1142 by Payen le Bouteiller, lord of Montréal and of the province of Oultre Jourdain. He made Kerak the new capital of the province, for it was superbly situated on the King's Highway, where it could control all traffic from north and south and grow rich by the imposition of road-tolls.

There were — as there are today — two parts of Kerak, both contained within stout walls, but the citadel and its fortress are separated from the town by a deep dry moat (*clearly visible in the main photograph*). The fortress is typically Crusader, with dimly lit stone-vaulted rooms and corridors leading into each other through heavy arches and doorways (*below*).

All the inhabitants of the town could gather for protection within the citadel in times of danger — as they did in 1173 when the Zengid ruler Nur al-Din attacked the castle. His siege was unsuccessful, as were later attempts by Salah al-Din in 1183 (when the marriage of the heir of Kerak was taking place inside, and Salah al-Din chivalrously kept his siege-engines off the bridal tower), and again in 1184. It was not until the end of 1188, after a siege of more than a year, that Kerak finally surrendered to the Arabs. The last lord of Kerak, the perfidious Renaud de Chatillon, was executed by Salah al-Din himself.

In 1263 the Mamluk Sultan Baybars took Kerak and destroyed the Church of Nazareth. The Arab traveller Ibn Battuta, who visited in 1355, was much impressed by the castle's strength, and said that it was also called 'The Castle of the Raven'. Under the Ottomans it was ruled by local families until 1840, when Ibrahim Pasha, son of Muhammad Ali of Egypt, took it, greatly damaging its defences. After the First World War, Kerak was a British administrative centre until the Emirate of Transjordan was established in 1921. It remains the centre of a large district.

Kerak is still a largely Christian town, and many of today's Christian families trace their origins back to the Byzantines.

# INDEX

**Abbasid dynasty** 10, 25
**Abdullah, Emir** 10, 13
**Ajlun** 18
**Alexander Jannaeus** 20, 25, 42
**Ali, Emir** 10
**Amareen** 52
**Amman** 13, 14
**Ammon** 8, 10, 13
**Amorites** 38
**Antigonus the One-eyed, King** 9
**Antioch on the Chrysorhoas** 16
**Aqaba** 56
**Arab Legion** 10
**Arab Revolt** 28, 54, 56
**Arabia, Province of** 10, 28, 44
**Arabian Oryx** 28
**Aretas III Philhellene, King** 46
**Assyrians** 9
**Aybak ibn Abd Allah** 18
**Azraq Oasis** 28
**Azraq Wetlands Reserve** 28
**Azz al-Din Ausama** 18
**Azz al-Din Aybak** 28

**Bashan** 13
**Bdoul** 52
**Bedouin** 30, 42, 52
**Bedouin Police** 54
**breadmaking** 52
**Burckhardt, John** 8, 46, 48
**Burgon, Dean** 48
**Byzantines** 26

**Constantine, Emperor** 10
**Crusaders** 8, 10, 18, 59, 62

**Damascus** 9
**Dana** 61
**Dana Wildlife Reserve** 61
**David, King** 9
**Dead Sea** 8, 40
**Decapolis** 10, 13, 16, 20, 25
**Deir** 50

**East Ghor Canal Project** 22
**Edom** 8, 44, 56
**Egeria** 40
**Exodus** 38

**Feisal, Emir** 10, 56
*fellahin* 61

**Gadara** 20
**Gerasa** 16
**Ghor** 22
**Gilead, hills of** 16, 22
**Glubb Pasha** 10, 54

**Hejaz railway** 10, 13
**Herod Antipas** 42
**Herod the Great** 10, 13, 26, 42
**Herodias** 42
**Horns of Hattin** 18
**Hussein, King** 10, 11
**Hussein ibn Ali, Sherif** 10

**Jebel Amman** 14
**Jebel Jofeh** 14
**Jerash** 16
**Jesus** 20
**John the Baptist** 42
**Jordan, river** 8
**Jordan Valley** 22, 25

**Kerak** 38, 62
**King's Highway** 8, 59
**Kir-haraseth** 62
**Koran** 32

**Lawrence, T.E.** 10, 28, 54, 56
**Lear, Edward** 48

**Machaerus** 42
**Madaba** 38
**Mark Antony** 10
**Meleager** 20
**Mesha** 38
**Mesha Stele** 38
**Moab** 8
**Moabite Stone** 38
**Moses** 8, 40
**Mukawir** 42
**Musil, Alois** 30, 32, 56

**Nabataeans** 9, 10, 13, 26, 42, 44, 46, 50, 54, 56
**Nebo, Mount** 40
**Nebuchadnezzar, King** 13, 44
**Nur al-Din** 62

**Og, King** 13
**olive cultivation** 22
**Ottoman Empire** 10

**Palestinians** 14
**Pella** 25
**Peraea** 10, 42
**Peter the Iberian** 40
**Petra** 10, 44, 46, 48, 50
**Philadelphia** 13, 14
**Pompey** 10
**Ptolemy II Philadelphus** 9, 13

**Qala'at al-Rabadh** 18
**Qasr al-Kharaneh** 34
**Qasr al-Mushatta** 36
**Qasr al-Tuba** 30
**Qasr Amra** 32

**Rabbah** 13
**Roberts, David** 8, 48

**Sala al-Din** 10, 18, 56, 59, 62
**Salome** 42
**Saul, King** 9
**Save the Children** 42
**Seetzen, Jasper** 16
**Seleucus** 9
**Septimius Severus** 28
**Shaumari Wildlife Reserve** 28
**sheep-farming** 22
**Shobak Castle** 59
**Siq** 44, 46
**Siyagha** 40
**Solomon, King** 56

**Tabaqat Fahl** 25
**Talal, King** 11
**Trajan, Emperor** 10
**Transjordan** 10, 56

**Umayyad dynasty** 10
**Umm al-Jimal** 26
**Umm Qeis** 20, 22
**Urban Development Department** 14

**Wadi Arabah** 44, 56, 61
**Wadi Mousa** 44, 46
**Wadi Rum** 54
**Wadi Sirhan** 28
**Walid I, Caliph** 32, 34
**Walid II, Caliph** 30, 36
**West Bank** 10, 11

**Yarmouk, river** 10, 20

22